A Chorus Of Lost Dreams

A collection of poems - Stories of women's fate that are often buried or left untold.

Aanchal Gupta

BookLeaf Publishing

India | USA | UK

Made with ❤ on the BookLeaf Publishing Platform
www.bookleafpub.in
www.bookleafpub.com

Dedication

For my grandparents,
whose love has been my foundation
and whose wisdom lights my way.
I hope your strength, kindness, and endless warmth
will live on in every word I write.

Preface

This collection of poems is a tribute to the countless
women whose stories are often left untold or unheard.
Women who have navigated through life's challenges
not just because of fate, but because of the expectations
and limitations society has placed upon them. These
poems are tales of resilience, quiet rebellion, and the
unbreakable spirit of those who have endured hardships
simply for being women.

Each piece in this book draws inspiration from the lived
experiences of women—those who have fought to be
heard, those who have struggled against the constraints
of societal norms, and those who have quietly defied the
roles assigned to them. These are not stories of victims
but of survivors, of women who, despite being silenced,
fought for their rights and happiness.

Through these poems, I hope to capture the essence of
their strength, their pain, their courage, and their joy. I
want these words to serve as both a reflection of their
battles and a celebration of their victories, however small
or grand they may be.

This book is for every woman who has been told to be

less, to dream smaller, to stay silent, or to shrink into the background. May these poems remind us of all that within every struggle, there is power, and within every woman, there is a story worth telling.

Acknowledgements

To all the poets and writers whose words have inspired me along the way, thank you for reminding me of the beauty of language and the power of expression.

And most importantly, to every reader who picks up this book, thank you for allowing my words to become a part of your world. It is for you that these poems were written, and I hope they resonate with you as deeply as they did with me.

1. A Girl I Am

A girl I am, and blissfully so,
Unfazed by whispers that ebb and flow.
For those who speak, their hearts are cold,
Indifference cloaked in tales retold.

No intent to wound, no wish to mar,
I seek to chart my course, my star.
In shadows cast by judgment's gaze,
I long to live, unfurl my ways.

Mistakes loom large, year after year,
For perfection's weight brings naught but fear.
Though faultless hearts are oft betrayed,
Blame finds a home, it's a silent charade.

What ghosts haunt, what phantoms fume?
What sins were committed before the womb?
Each twist of fate, a bitter jest,
Rules forged in fire, yet we're oppressed.

We crafted chains, then dread their break,
The illusion of equality, a cruel mistake.
If change is life, a river's flow,
Why cling to shores where shadows grow?

2. A Distress Call

Old as time, this tale unwinds,
Women bear the weight of countless binds.
Expected to sacrifice, to bend and break,
Yet labeled fragile, for society's sake.

Through silent storms, we weather the pain,
Told to let go, to dance in the rain.
Still chaos surrounds, a constant embrace,
Cursed from the start, in this weary place.

In a world that shudders at our ascent,
We question the chains, the silence, the rent.
How we whisper, we wail, our voices entwined,
But in the stillness, our spirits confined.

What then, dear world, when dreams are suppressed?
Why does our flight leave you so distressed?

3. A Cheap Shot

She whispers, in the night of the dark,
Yearning for a miraculous arc.
Though the truth shines bright, a victim's sigh,
She must bear the weight of being the fall guy.

If she falters, if her voice trembles slight,
Labeled a liar, a witch of the night.
Not crimes we commit, just boundaries we draw,
Resisting the wants that twist and withdraw.

Perhaps we wear a cloak of cautious fears,
Yet better that than drown in bitter tears.
For to live in the light of false dreams' embrace,
Is to wander a path not meant for her grace.

They say we complain, that we have enough,
But who decides worth in this game of the tough?
Who said we are what and what we are not,
Why does this distinction feel like a cheap shot?

4. A Change of Heart

Skepticism lingers, our claims called far-fetched,
But what else was to expect?
If past whispers faded into silence,
Why should we not scream in defiance?

Anger, a weighty shroud, and guilt, an unwelcome guest,
We bear chilling tales of human-interest.
Monsters here do not lurk beneath the bed,
As they fear the wrath of a man's thick head.

Women are mere tokens, broken and bespoken,
Such are the tales that haunt us awoken.
Evil ignites like a wildfire, swift and coward,
All to prevent us from moving forward.

We abandon the path of begging and retreat,
We have embraced standing on our own feet.
For the world must finally heed the wails,
That are hidden behind silenced veils.

5. A Tale of Two Shores

In shadows cast by a dimming sun,
A little girl dwelt, where hope was undone.
On a tiny isle, where the winds whispered low,
Her family struggled, in sorrow's heavy flow.

Her mother, frail as the autumn leaves,
Lay in a bed woven with silent grieves.
Her father, trapped by the bottle's cruel embrace,
Stumbled through life, lost in a haze.

Yet the girl, with hands both tender and worn,
Dared to dream, have hopes that lingered, forlorn.
She gathered the crops, a harvest of pain,
With strength in her heart, she bore the strain.

Oh, how she yearned for the world beyond,
To heal her mother, to renew their bond.
Under streetlights, where shadows would dance,
She learned and spurned, lost in a trance.

But laughter rang out, sharp as a blade,
"Foolish child!" they taunted, "Your hopes will fade."
Her mother, burdened, with little to say,
And a father, transformed by the drink's cruel sway.

One fateful night, from corners where nightmares reside,
A monster emerged, with malice as guide.
The devil approached, with gold in his grip,
A bargain so vile, a treacherous slip.

"To sell her," he whispered, "to serve on the other shore,
Where wealth cloaks the heart, and kindness is poor."
Fear wrapped around her like chains of despair,
The girl felt the darkness, the weight of the air.

As she turned to leave with the man,
His gaze cold and sly, it all felt like a scam.
He beckoned with malice, a sinister scheme,
Leering with intentions that made her insides scream.

6. A Sibling Rivalry

In a quiet house, a father bore the weight,
Two children, a son and daughter, his fate.
Their mother, lost to time's cruel embrace,
Whispered a wish, a dream they would chase.

"Let her stand tall, a beacon of light,
In a world that confines, let her take flight."
But society scoffed, called her an outcast,
For seeking knowledge, for breaking the cast.

Together they fought, as hardship lingered near,
To honor the mother's wish, to conquer their fear.
Alas! Love's tangled web wove a tragic thread,
When the son fell for a maiden, where tradition was
bred.
He asked her father for her hand in marriage,
He was shunned, labeled a savage.

"Your sister is a disgrace to our society," he said,
"If you come near my daughter again, you will be on

your deathbed."
In rage and desperation, blind in love, the son struck a
blow,
The world anyway wasn't ready for his sister's glow.

Drenched in her blood, an offering to behold,
He sought the father-in-law to claim his marital gold.
And lo, the man smiled, he found a worthy groom,
Not afraid to do what needs to be done, with no gloom.

There was no shock, no grief, just cold, empty eyes,
A girl dared to be different, and now here she lies.

7. A Carnival of Sorts

In twilight's embrace, I wandered astray,
Stumbling upon a village, lost in dismay.
Its streets whispered secrets, shadows held tight,
The townsfolk, hesitant, cloaked in the night.
They granted us refuge, yet warned of the dark,
"Stay in, for the night holds a perilous spark."

Within four walls, we sought to find repose,
But curiosity, like wildfire, arose.
In shadows deep, we broke the silent pact,
Mistaking joy for something abstract.
We thought it a festival, laughter in air,
Yet beneath the bright colors, a sinister snare.

Women, like treasures, marked with cruel price,
Traded like whispers, a fate far from nice.
Their glances caught ours, a warning unspun,
And in that brief moment, our fate done.

A rush of cold strike, with darkness consumed,

We awoke in a hospital, bruised and entombed.
Now haunted by visions of those faces so grim,
Each night they linger, their hopes growing dim.
In dreams, I still wander, wishing them free,
For every lost voice echoed, a plea to be.

8. A Father's Wish

A girl once wove her dreams with threads of gold,
Into a family of honor, her father's wish foretold.
A naive princess, wrapped in silken care,
Accepted a stranger, with a heart unaware.

Her father, with hope, passed the weight of his pride,
To a groom bound by duty, yet longing to hide.
For the heart of this man belonged to another's grace,
But at the altar, he wore a reluctant face.

After vows were whispered, he slipped from her side,
His mother's sweet lies cloaked the truth he would bide.
She believed in the tale that he toiled day and night,
Unaware of the deceit that lingered out of sight.

Then fate cast its shadow, as sorrow claimed her kin,
Her mother departed, leaving silence within.
Returning from mourning, a scene pierced her heart,
Her husband entwined with another, torn apart.

In panic, she stumbled, her world spun away,
Down the stairs, she fell, where hopes lay in dismay.
Now three years have passed, in her father's embrace,
Yet he questions the lessons that left such a trace:
"What fault lies in raising a daughter to stand,
To navigate storms with her own steady hand?"

9. A Fairytale Ending

In the lap of opulence, my father thrived,
A king of soirées, where laughter jived,
While my mother, Stoic, slipped from his gaze,
Two hearts entwined in a mutual haze.

Their disdain, a river, flowed deep and wide,
Only for the twins, they ever tried.
Born when I was but five springs old,
In the attic I languished, a story untold.

A mansion of grandeur, the largest of all,
And I, a girl, banished from sight, a mere ghost in the
halls.
For I was unwanted, a shame cloaked in gloom,
While my brothers, like jewels, danced in their bloom.

Adored and indulged, they played in the sun,
While I feasted on silence, my battles unwon.
In pages of stories, my spirit took flight,
In a realm of my making, I found my own light.

Until came the day, and I was drenched in sin.
An accusation, a whisper, against my own kin.
Defending my haven, my fortress, my right,
How could I know he was blood alright?

A brother's intrusion, a stranger unknown,
In defense, I acted, shattering his bones.
"Madness," they murmur, "from solitude's grasp,"
In a cage for my sanity, they tighten their clasp.

In this new prison, my stories remain with me,
Within these walls, my spirit still roams free.

10. A Love Story

In a village torn by faith's cruel divide,
Two sects stood firm; their hearts filled with pride.
No mingling allowed no bridge to span,
A simmering hatred, a bitter clan.

Yet love, a wildflower in the cracks,
Bloomed between a girl and boy, hearts unshackled.
In secret whispers, their attraction took flight,
But darkness loomed, shadows of the night.

To escape the chains of their fateful ties,
They fled the watchful, judgmental eyes.
But irony danced in the moon's pale glow,
For the feuding sects found a common foe.

With enmity cast aside, they joined as one,
Pursuing the lovers, their mission begun.
In unity forged from hatred's deep well,
Together they hunted, together they quell.

Oh, if only they'd banded for love's gentle call,
The village might thrive, no longer to stall.
But alas, they chose evil, to silence the light,
While love, like a whisper, faded from sight.

11. A Divine Blessing

In a town where darkness danced with pride,
A curious ritual unfolded, side by side.
The eldest daughter, upon her coming of age,
Was adorned like a goddess, the town's gilded page.

Draped in finery, her beauty unveiled,
In the heart of the town, her worth was regaled.
Men from afar, with eager intent,
Came to judge her spirit, her presence to rent.

A parade of desire, a spectacle grand,
They reached out, they teased, with a sly, eager hand.
The daughters were deemed as treasures to share,
Meant to please the beholders, they had no prayer.

With pride, families cherished this fate,
As fathers orchestrated, sealing their kin's state.
For the legacy born from numbers and guise,
Masked the truth lurking beneath veiled skies.

Unseen were the chains that bound them in place,
These girls, born as harlots, knew not their own grace.
In a world crafted solely for others' delight,
They danced in the darkness, forsaking their light.

12. A Price to Pay

Once, beneath the waves, a sea witch dwelled,
Her heart fed on the whispers of girls, compelled
By a world that scoffed at their tender grace,
Mocked their reflections, teased their true face.

From kingdoms afar, on the edge of despair,
They sought her enchantments, a magical snare.
With tales woven deep, she spun her delight,
But one summer's tale danced in the moonlight.

A distant prince, with vanity crowned,
Sailed to a realm where dreams swirled around.
Fair maidens, enchanted by his fleeting glance,
Yearned to be princesses, to capture romance.

"His heart seeks the fair," one girl dared to say,
"Yet another whispered, 'Only the thin shall sway.'"
But fickle as tides, his desires would shift,
And the girls, ever hopeful, would seek the sea witch's
gift.

They traded their essence for beauty's cruel dream,
Unraveling slowly, like threads of a seam.
As summer waned, they gazed in despair,
Their faces a canvas, worn thin by the air.

Once vibrant and fresh, now haggard and stale,
They lost what was precious in pursuit of their tale.
And the prince, like a shadow, slipped quietly away,
Leaving hearts heavy, as night swallowed day.

To another kingdom, he ventured alone,
While the sea witch collected the seeds he had sown.
In the depths of her lair, the echoes would ring—
Beauty's cruel price, a most sorrowful thing.

13. A Holy Matrimony

Once upon a time, they whispered in soft tones,
A voice like honey, a melody, it deserves to be honed.
Neighbors would marvel, "Such raw talent shines!"
In the cradle of song, my desire intertwined.

Joy danced in my chest, a sweet serenade,
Dreams of a world, where my voice would cascade.
My father, with pride, would beam like the sun,
An angel's face paired with a voice that could stun.

"Such splendid pedigree," he mused with delight,
Searching through kingdoms, seeking a suitor just right.
My gift turned to currency, a jewel on display,
To barter my spirit, like a price to pay.

He found me a husband, a match, strong and true,
And content in my silence, I wore my facade blue.
But in quiet moments, a shadow draws near,
A whisper of longing, a flicker of fear.

Am I merely existing, a breath without song?
Has the dream of my youth faded, where did I go wrong?
In the halls of matrimony, did I trade my bright light,
For a life that is safe but shrouded in night?

14. A Nightmarish Dream

She wed a man, not deemed good by gentle eyes,
A tyrant cloaked in familiar guise.
He wields his love like chains that bind,
With harsh words, he carves her heart, unkind.

Yet in shadows, she whispers, "Is this the norm?"
Her mother bore this storm, her friends too, worn.
Who else but she must bear the weight,
Of his unyielding fury, his twisted trait.

At times, a flicker, a thought to flee,
But where do I wander, who waits for me?
No refuge to claim, my past a tight bind,
Each thread of my life, a memory confined.

A brave friend once rose, defied the decree,
But silence was met with a harsh penalty.
Her voice, a crime, had the men outraged,
The defiance and her will deserved to be caged.

While her husband roamed free,
Unbothered, unshackled, disengaged with glee.
What justice was this, I wondered,
Where the victim's pain was considered a burden.

Ah, to be a man, where freedom's a right,
While she languishes, dreaming of light.
In a world where silence is all I can keep,
I ache for the courage to wake from this sleep.

15. A Rare Find

In the quiet burdens of duty,
She learned the art of the kitchen's embrace.
To stir the pot of expectation,
To sweeten the taste of her husband's brace.

With hands that toiled through chores,
she perfected all that she was told,
For who else would tend to the hearth—
bare the wrath of the burning coal.

Education slipped like shadows, a distant, fading light,
Her role etched in tradition, a reminder, always in sight.
"Learn to please a man, what else is there to do?" they
asked,
A mantra of servitude, a burden attached.

And the day finally came, the crown of her fate,
To be a Mrs., a lady, the pride of the estate.
But what is a title when the heart feels no glee?
A husband, a fortune, but who is he to me?

Born with silver spoons, his vanity aglow,
And in his rudeness, all warmth seemed to go.
She strained, and she labored, day turned into night,
For was it her onus to chase away the blight?

For all the journeys her husband took, for all he had
seen,
Could he not learn kindness, perhaps a gentler routine?
He is supposed to be Worldly, a man ahead of his times,
A decent human being, perhaps the rarest find.

16. A Myth of Miracle

A deep silence reigned, here wild vines entwine,
A jungle breathes, a realm of artificial design.
Its heart whispers tales of woe,
A place where light seldom dares to go.

And beside this thicket, a town stands bright,
A curious haven, where joy feels right.
Yet in this laughter, a strange tune plays,
For here, boys are born, to the sun's warm rays.

A magic lures souls from lands afar,
To test their fate beneath the evening star.
They seek a blessing, a son to hold,
In this sanctuary, where legends unfold.

But beneath the smiles, a shadow casts,
For joy is laced with a sorrow that lasts.
The jungle cradles whispers of girls' unseen,
Buried in dirt, their unborn presence, so lean, pristine.

Not our fault, it is the kin's despair,
Chasing a boy in a world unfair.
Their love a currency, traded with grief,
In the quest for a son, they find no relief.

Alas, no magic is woven, only curses are stolen,
A tale of longing, a desire to have pride swollen.
The screams of the daughters are drowned in woe,
as a boy is what they need to sow.

In the quest for a legacy, they turn a blind eye,
The facade of luck, nothing but a lie.
Killing comes easy, when humanity goes rogue,
There's a jungle next to this town, a grove of lost souls.

17. A Peculiar Freedom

Born into a realm of gilded dreams,
Where treasures flowed like rivers,
And every wish was an easy breeze.

Adored, I bloomed like a rare flower,
Their little princess, a testament of love,
Nestled in the embrace of safety's tower.

But whispers warned of shadows lurking,
"Keep her close, shield her light,
For fortuity is a fragile thing,
Too precious for the night."

Like porcelain, I sat, a delicate prize,
Hidden from the world's watchful eyes.
In this sanctuary, my heart did confine,
With promises that no man would ever claim.

And as the day turned to dusk,
I gazed through glass, yearning for the wild,

The moon a distant friend,
A silent call to the untamed.

Each night, I ponder, a soul in a cell,
What is wealth if freedom's price is steep?
In the stillness, I find my truth,
In shadows cast by love's fierce keep.
A heart that craves the open skies,
Yearns to soar, to break these ties.

18. A Deadly Storm

In shadows cast, we bore the name,
Untouchables, marked by whispered shame.
Villagers turned, like leaves from the storm,
In this new world, the old scars still warm.

Our kin, a tapestry of humble thread,
Grateful for scraps, yet longing for bread.
We toiled in silence, our backs bent low,
The more we complied, the harsher their woe.

And then one night when the heavens did weep,
As homes crumbled, and silence fell deep,
A shelter stood tall, yet barred was the way,
"Let them be lost," the cruel voices say.

Drenched and forsaken, we fought through the night,
Against rain and fury, we clung to the light.
Our worth was like the litter, so easily tossed,
In this world, our lives will never have a cost.

Fate, a cruel script, penned long before,
In the grip of despair, we knock at death's door.
And now a hope, a faint glimmer, whispers its plea,
Wherever it leads us, may we finally be free.

19. A Lack of Choice

Born in trenches, a father so poor,
Our mother departed, leaving dreams at the door.
With hopes in my heart, I longed to lend aid,
Yet to marriage market's gate, my father paraded.

Born a girl, I was a burden, a weight father had to bear,
And choices were shackled, my voice lost in this lair.
His gaze fixed on suitors, their eyes on my worth,
Beauty, the currency, my only rebirth.

So, I polished my soul, like a gem so bright,
An ideal wife crafted, a beauty that excites.
And how well it paid off, I found a husband who was just
right.
For years no trauma, I found my own space.

In a fate sought by many, I learned to endure,
A whisper of freedom, though never secure.
My husband, a phantom, barely glanced my way,
They whispered his motives, child-bearer at bay.

My life of empty struggle, my presence won't be missed,
The scar is deep, not a lover, not a friend, I was mere
mist.
But in this strange land, where choices are few,
I found solace in silence, a life without rue.

For men make their choices, with power in hand,
While I, just a vessel, in this intricate plan.

20. A New Dream

In the tender bloom of childhood's grace,
I was told of dreams, something I could chase.
With tools in hand, a heart so bold,
I was promised the world, a future to behold.

Yet at twenty, the winds shifted, a storm born of fate,
"Marriage awaits," they said, "it's time to navigate."
I turned to my father, with hope in my plea,
"What of my dreams? Do they still live in me?"

"It's not mine to decide," he replied with a sigh,
"You're woven now, into another's sky."
So, I donned the mantle, a bride in the fray,
As the echoes of longing began to fade day by day.

Time a construct, passed by slow, my spirit grew dim,
The dreams grew slim, reduced to a silly whim.
"Learn to cook, learn to clean," the chorus would sing,
"A wife should be a keeper, aim for that ring."

And if children don't come, what then would I be?
A hollow reflection of lost reverie.
I bowed to the pressure, to the life I was shown,
A future painted bright, yet so falsely grown.

But now in her laughter, my daughter ignites,
A fire untamed, a spirit that fights.
She needs no permission, her wings spread wide,
Together we'll chase every dream she decides.

For when she looks back, may she see clear,
The echoes of freedom, the dreams that endear.
In her heart, I'll plant seeds of desire,
To soar through the heavens, unbound and inspired.

21. A Tale She Wove

In every age, the evil enchants,
Where greed entwines with disgrace's glance.
A monster lurks in every nook,
Its hunger vast, a treacherous book.

They cloak it in rules, in tradition's guise,
A veil for the crimes beneath their lies.
By day, they roam, unmasked, yet unseen,
These specters of power, so cruel, so mean.

We witness the scars, the echoes of plight,
Their hollow excuses, devoid of light.
We feel their intent, dark whispers that creep,
Yet we turn our backs, as if lost in sleep.

We feel the wounds they carve, spun us with lies,
Ignited by the malice lurking behind hollowed eyes.
But we, the haunted, refuse to turn away,
For our stories echo, haunting light of day.

No longer shall we hide, nor burden our scars with
shame,
We rise to make the world behold and call out each
monster's name.